FACE TO FACE WITH
ORANGUTANS

by Tim Laman
and Cheryl Knott

NATIONAL
GEOGRAPHIC

WASHINGTON, D.C.

FACE TO FACE

← *One day when it started to rain, this big orangutan we call Jari Manis used a leafy branch as an umbrella to keep his head dry. "Jari manis" means "ring finger" in the Indonesian language. We named him this because he is missing part of his finger.*

It's not easy to get face to face with a wild orangutan. For one thing, orangutans spend most of their time high in the trees. Also, they are usually afraid of people. But one day in the rain forest of Borneo, I got lucky.

For weeks, I had been following a big male orangutan we call Jari Manis. He had gotten more and more used to me as he saw me following him every day, but he usually stayed up in the trees and kept his distance. Then one day he spotted

MONKEY OR APE?

■ Orangutans are great apes, like their close relatives, gorillas and chimpanzees. Monkeys are a different kind of primate.

■ Apes don't have tails, but monkeys do.

■ Apes are bigger than monkeys and have broad chests.

■ Apes have large brains and are very intelligent. They are more similar to humans than they are to monkeys. They are our closest relatives.

a treat on the ground that he couldn't resist—a termite nest. Orangutans love to eat termites. He cautiously came down and started feeding, ignoring me. He broke off chunks of nest and sucked out the termites. Yum!

I was there with my camera to record it all. I slowly moved in as close as I dared. I was less than 30 feet (9 m) away from him—the closest I had ever been to a wild orangutan. With my telephoto lens on my camera, I was able to get a close-up of Jari's face.

After Jari finished his termite breakfast, he sat down for a little rest. It started to rain, and then the most amazing thing happened. Do you know what he did? He grabbed some leafy branches from a small tree next to him, and held them over his head to block the rain. He had made an umbrella! That made me realize how smart orangutans are.

Local people realized long ago how similar orangutans were to people. In fact, in the Indonesian language, "orang" means "person," and "Hutan" means "forest." So the word "orangutan" means "person of the forest."

As Jari sat there with his leafy umbrella over his head, he looked toward me and our eyes met. It wasn't like looking into the eyes of other animals. It gave me a different feeling, like he was thinking about me. I wondered if Jari knew that his rain forest home was shrinking and that humans were the problem. Maybe not, but I decided right then that I wanted to use my pictures and stories to teach people about orangutans and about saving their rain forest home.

⬆ *Holding chunks of a termite nest, Jari Manis sucks the termites out of the hollow spaces inside.*

MEET

This pregnant female orangutan needs to eat a lot of ripe fruits to nourish her growing baby.

THE ORANGUTAN

Orangutans make a new nest to sleep in almost every night. I climbed about 40 feet (12 m) up a nearby tree to get this shot of a male sitting in his nest before he went to sleep.

When I was a boy, I loved to climb trees, and I thought I was pretty good at it. But on my first trip to Borneo, I saw a wild orangutan climbing and clambering from one tree to the next, quickly cruising through the canopy. I realized I was a pretty lousy climber compared to him.

Since that first trip more than 20 years ago, I have been to Borneo many times. For several years, I lived in the rain forest doing research and photography. Working closely with my wife, Cheryl,

9

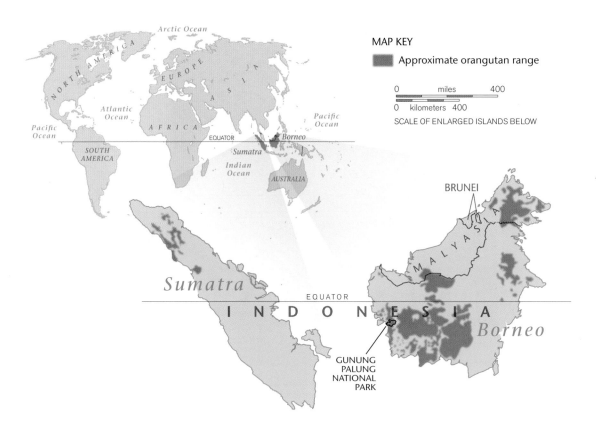

MAP KEY

Approximate orangutan range

0   miles   400
0   kilometers 400
SCALE OF ENLARGED ISLANDS BELOW

↑ *There are two kinds, or species, of orangutans. One species is found on the island of Borneo. The other species lives on the island of Sumatra. The orangutans shown in this book live in Borneo's Gunung Palung National Park.*

who is an orangutan researcher, I have had a chance to learn a lot about orangutans.

The only places in the world that wild orangutans live are the rain forests of two big tropical islands called Borneo and Sumatra, in the countries of Indonesia and Malaysia.

Orangutans spend most of their lives in the trees. They eat in the trees, travel through the trees, and even sleep in the trees. They really

⬇ *In just one day, an orangutan can eat many different kinds of rain forest fruits. These are just some of the fruits they like.*

⬆ This young male orang-utan is eating seeds high up in a giant rain forest tree called a dipterocarp (which means "two-winged fruit" in Latin). You can see the big red wings attached to the seeds—kind of like a maple seed, but much bigger.

depend on trees for their survival.

Orangutans have many special features that make them good climbers. They have long arms that give them extra reach. They have really long fingers to grab on to big branches. Their big toes work like thumbs, so they can also grab branches with their feet. It's like having an extra pair of hands!

The main reason that orangutans need to be such good tree climbers is because that's

→ *Sometimes Cheryl climbs up to the canopy so she can see the forest from an orangutan's point of view.*

HOW TO SPEAK ORANGUTAN

Orangutans make sounds to communicate. Scientists have funny names for the sounds, like "gorkum," "lork," and "grumph." Here are a few examples:

— Angry orangutans make a loud "kiss-squeak" sound. You can do this by kissing the back of your hand as loud as you can.

— Big males make a long call so others know they are near. It starts with a deep burbling sound and then turns into long booming calls.

— Young orangutans sometimes whimper to call for their moms.

where they find most of their food. Orangutans eat over a hundred different kinds of fruits. They also eat many nuts. But even in the rain forest, they can't always find their favorite foods. Sometimes they can't find any trees with fruit. Then they eat leaves or the inside part of tree bark. Special treats like termite nests are high-protein snacks.

Bananas are one fruit you won't see wild orangutans eating. Bananas don't grow in the rain forest where orangutans live. So if you ever see a picture of an orangutan eating a banana, you know the orangutan is probably in a zoo or was given the banana by a human.

To learn more about orangutans, Cheryl collects some of their urine (better known as pee). This can be a little tricky to do, because they're up in the

trees, and you are down below. You don't want to be peed on by an orangutan! Since orangutans sleep in trees, the secret is to put a plastic sheet under their nest early in the morning. Then, when they wake up and pee, you can catch some of it on the plastic. Cheryl later examines the urine to see if the animal is healthy or if a female is pregnant.

This wide-eyed young orangutan is about one year old.

ORANGUTAN LIFE

This infant orangutan is only a few weeks old. Even newborns are strong enough to hang on to Mom with their hands and feet while she moves through the trees.

Orangutans have pretty big bellies, so it is often hard to tell if a female is pregnant just by looking at her. But one day, Cheryl tested an orangutan's urine and found out she was pregnant.

Having a baby is a rare event in an orangutan's life. A mother orangutan needs to keep nursing her baby for many years and has to carry it all day. So she can't have a second baby until the first one is about eight years old and can travel on its own. No other mammal takes so much time between babies.

Baby orangutans cling to mom at first. Then they start moving about on their own. They learn how to use the vines and branches that surround them in the rain forest—their very own jungle gym.

We followed the pregnant female every day so we could see her baby when it was born. It was hard to keep up with her. She traveled farther and farther from our camp, and we had to hike a long way in the dark every morning to get to her nest. One day it rained so much that the streams flooded, and we had to wade through water up to our chests to get back to our camp. Finally, one day she hid so well up in a big tree that we lost track of her. The next time we saw her several days later, she had a brand new little baby clinging to her.

Females raise their babies all by themselves. The females have to nurse the babies and travel around the forest looking for fruit to eat. Unlike their ape relatives, the chimpanzees and gorillas, orangutans don't live in groups. Except for the moms, who stay with their babies, both females and males are mostly solitary. They live on their own in the forest.

Orangutans do occasionally meet other orangutans, though. Sometimes, if a really big tree has lots of fruit, a bunch of orangutans will gather to eat. Females will sometimes hang out there and even travel together, especially if they are related.

There are two types of adult males, big males

← *A mother orangutan can have a young baby and also an older brother or sister. They stay with the mother until they are between 8 and 12 years old. For this orangutan family, it's nap time.*

HOW TO STUDY ORANGUTANS

It takes many days of searching the forest to find an orangutan. Here are some of the things you need to do:

▬ Hike through thick forests, wade through swamps, and climb steep hills. If it starts raining, put on your poncho and keep going.

▬ Watch orangutans with your binoculars.

▬ Take lots of notes about everything the orangutans do.

▬ Get up before it's light so you can get to their nest before they wake up.

This large male orangutan is in his prime. He has the big cheek pads and throat pouch that only some adult males develop.

(the ones with cheek pads) and small males. All males start out as small males. Some develop cheek pads and become big males right away. Others stay small for many years, and some may never become big males. Scientists are still trying to figure out why this is. It's possible that by staying small, the small males can avoid conflict with other males.

These small males sometimes form little gangs that roam from place to place. The big males don't like each other at all. A big male sometimes gets into a fight with another male to stop him from mating with the females in that area. Males will hit, bite, and wrestle with each other in the trees or on the ground. Sometimes they get injured from these fights, so the life of a big male is a rough one.

Scientists are still learning about orangutans. For instance, we have found that orangutans have different habits, depending on where they live. They may eat the same foods but in different ways. Some use sticks as tools, but others don't. In some places orangutans make pillows and blankets out of leaves. Just as people in different places learn customs from the people around them, orangutans learn things from the other orangutans in their area.

THE FUTURE

For many years, we have worked in a national park in Borneo called Gunung Palung. Our research camp is a whole day's journey up a small river, deep in the rain forest. It is usually a peaceful place. But one day, we heard a strange noise in the distance. It was the roar of chain saws echoing through the forest. People were not supposed to be cutting trees inside the park, but they were doing it anyway.

Logging is a huge problem for orangutans in many parts of Borneo and Sumatra because it destroys

Logging is a huge problem for orangutans because it destroys their forest home. These logs in Borneo have been cut and then pulled out of the forest on wooden tracks.

their forest habitat. Once a rain forest is logged, it is often burned and turned into an oil palm plantation or some other place where orangutans can't live. This is the biggest reason that the number of orangutans has been declining for many years.

Some people kill mother orangutans and take their babies to sell as pets. This is illegal. When local officials find these baby orangutans, they bring them to places called rehabilitation centers.

I visited one of these centers a few years ago. I was shocked at how many young orangutans they had. There were hundreds of them. And the sad thing is that the number of orangutans forced out of their forest homes keeps growing.

At rehabilitation centers, people raise the young orangutans. They try to teach the animals the skills they need to live in the forest. Hopefully, many of these orangutans will be able to live on

⬆ Rehabilitation centers like this one in Borneo can get crowded because there are so many orphan orangutans. This is a far cry from life in the wild.

their own one day, but it is hard to find areas of good forest to put them in. Also, it's difficult for people to teach them everything they need to know. Wild orangutans spend about ten years learning from their mothers what to eat and how to survive. A crash course at a rehab center can't fully prepare a young orangutan for life in the wild.

The illegal logging in Gunung Palung seriously damaged parts of the park. But thanks to efforts by the national parks office, the Indonesian government, and conservation groups, the logging has now mostly stopped. The park is much better protected. So there are signs of hope that rain forests can be saved.

To have a safe future, orangutans need large areas of forest where they can live in the wild. That's why we need to protect the rain forests. By doing that, we save not only the orangutans, but all the other plants and animals of the rain forest too. If we work together, we can do it!

HOW YOU CAN HELP

⬇ *An orangutan's hand looks a lot like a human hand.*

Orangutans live in rain forests that may be very far away from you, but you could be contributing to the destruction of these forests in ways you aren't even aware of.

▬When your parents buy products made of wood, such as furniture, ask them if the wood is certified as sustainable. This means that rain forests weren't destroyed to get the wood.

▬ Palm oil is used in many of the products we have in our homes. The demand for palm oil encourages loggers to clear the rain forests and plant palm trees instead. Look at your bag of cookies, your ice cream carton, and your shampoo to see if palm oil is used. Ask your parents to try to avoid these products.

▬You, your friends, and your parents can contribute to one of the organizations working to save orangutans in the wild. The National Geographic's Conservation Trust, the Orangutan Conservancy, the Borneo Orangutan Survival

Foundation, and the Sumatran Orangutan Conservation Programme are some of the groups helping orangutans. Even if you can only give a little, it will feel good to contribute. Organizations like the Gunung Palung Orangutan Conservation Program work with Indonesian children and adults to teach them to protect the rain forests that surround their villages. You can also give to a rehabilitation center that helps the babies who have lost their moms.

▬Many zoos have important partnerships with orangutan conservation organizations. When you visit these zoos, you help support conservation. Encourage zoos that don't have such programs to contribute to conservation efforts to save orangutans in the wild.

▬ Write to your representatives in Congress and tell them that you support legislation such as "the Great Ape Conservation Act." This act provides funding to organizations helping orangutans and other apes.

IT'S YOUR TURN

Your best bet to come face to face with an orangutan yourself is to visit one of the many zoos that care for these animals. If you're lucky, you might one day go to Indonesia or Malaysia and see an orangutan in the wild or at a rehabilitation center. Here are some ideas for ways that you can get closer to orangutans:

1 Visit a zoo with orangutans and plan on spending a good chunk of time at the orangutan exhibit. The longer you are there, the more likely you are to see some interesting behaviors. Have your camera ready!

2 Think about what is different about the behavior of orangutans you see in the zoo and what you've learned about wild orangutans. Would you see the same kind of social group in the wild? Are they sitting on the ground or up high? What are the orangutans eating? What are they spending most of their time doing?

3 When you see a movie or commercial that has an orangutan or other ape in it acting like a person, how does it make you feel? Are they showing how the orangutan really lives? Or are they making fun of orangutans by pretending the animals are like people? What do you think they had to do to get the orangutan to act like that?

4 Learn more about orangutans and the rain forest so you can tell people why it is important to protect them and their habitat. Find out about the different projects that study wild orangutans and about the organizations that are working to protect them.

It would be fun to be able to climb through the treetops like an orangutan.

FACTS AT A GLANCE

↓ *Orangutans' feet are different from humans' feet. An orangutan's big toe works like a thumb.*

Species

There are two species of orangutans living on different islands in Southeast Asia. The species living on Borneo is called *Pongo pygmaeus*. The species living on Sumatra is called *Pongo abelii*. They are very similar and were considered the same species until recently. In this book we talk about the Bornean orangutan.

Population

Today, fewer than 6,600 orangutans live in Sumatra and fewer than 54,000 live in Borneo. Orangutan populations are rapidly declining. Both orangutan species are endangered.

Types of males

There are two types of grown-up male orangutans. Big males are much larger, have cheek pads (also called cheek flanges), throat pouches, and make loud "long calls." Small males are smaller and do not have these special features. Small males may develop into big males, but some stay as small males for a long time. Scientists are still trying to learn more about these different types of males.

Size

Females weigh about 90 pounds (41 kg). Big males can weigh 180 pounds (82 kg) or more. Small males are about the size of females or a bit larger. Orangutans are about 4 to 4.5 feet (1-1.3 m) tall.

Lifespan

Orangutans can live to be over 50 years old. In the wild, it is probably more common to live to be 30 to 40 years old.

Special Features

Orangutans are the world's largest arboreal (or tree-living) animals. They have hip joints that are like our shoulder joints, so they can move their legs all around, the same way that we can move our arms. This means they can easily stretch between two trees. Orangutans, especially the big males, often travel by swaying a tree from side to side. Then, when they get far enough over, they grab the next tree and spring across. When a young orangutan comes across a gap in the trees that is too wide for him to cross, orangutan mothers sometimes use their bodies to make a bridge. The youngster then climbs across the mom to get to the next tree.

Sometimes there is a big fruiting season in the forest, called a mast fruiting. When this happens, the orangutans can eat so much fruit that they get fat. When there is not much to eat, they use up this fat for energy.

In some areas, orangutans use tools such as sticks to get seeds out of a certain fruit and to eat insects, but in other places, they don't. They also do other odd things, like making leaf pillows or blankets in their nests.

Habitat

Orangutans live in the tropical rain forests. They prefer to live in peat swamps and lowland forests. Sometimes they go into mountain forests. Orangutans, especially males, have large home ranges.

Food

Orangutans are known to eat hundreds of kinds of plants. They prefer to eat fruit, including seeds, when they can. They will eat leaves and the inside of tree bark when they can't find fruit. They also eat insects, especially termites, and flowers.

Reproduction

Orangutans give birth only once every eight years or so. This is the longest birth spacing of any mammal. Pregnancy lasts almost as long as in humans— eight and a half months. Both types of adult males, the big males and the small ones, can mate with females.

Social Habits

Orangutans are mostly solitary. This means they live alone, except for the mothers and their babies. The big males with cheek pads avoid each other. Sometimes they get into fights. They can even die from the wounds they get in these fights. At times, the small males travel together in groups. Occasionally, a few pairs of mothers and babies will feed together in large fruiting trees. If there is enough fruit to eat, small groups of related females will travel and eat together. In some places, orangutans can be much more social, probably because that place has more for them to eat.

Biggest Threats

Bornean orangutans are endangered, and Sumatran orangutans are critically endangered. Endangered means an animal faces a very high risk of becoming extinct in the wild. Critically endangered means the animal faces an extremely high risk of becoming extinct in the wild. The biggest threat is rain forest destruction caused by logging (both legal and illegal), conversion to oil palm plantations, fire, and mining. Orangutan mothers are also killed to obtain infants for the illegal pet trade. In some areas orangutans are hunted for food or killed for other purposes. Most orangutans live outside protected national parks, but threats exist even in areas that are protected.

GLOSSARY

Arboreal: Living in the trees.

Canopy: The top level of the forest.

Clambering: Using both your hands and feet to climb; scrambling.

Endangered: A species with very few individuals remaining. If the number of individuals rises, the species classification may change to "threatened" or "recovered." If the number falls, the species may become "extinct," meaning no individuals remain.

Habitat: The place where a plant or animal naturally lives.

Mammals: Air-breathing, warm-blooded animals with hair whose offspring nurse on their mother's milk. Orangutans and humans are two kinds of mammals.

Rain forest: A dense forest with over 100 inches of rain per year.

Rehabilitation: Preparing an animal to survive in the wild after it has spent time in captivity.

Species: A group of animals or plants that look similar, can breed with one another, and have offspring who can also breed successfully.

FIND OUT MORE

Books & Articles

Knott, Cheryl & Tim Laman. "Orangutans in the Wild," *National Geographic* magazine, August 1998.

Knott, Cheryl & Tim Laman. "Orangutans Hang Tough," *National Geographic* magazine, October 2003.

Lumry, Amanda, and Laura Hurwitz. *Adventures of Riley: Operation Orangutan.* Bellevue, WA: Eaglemont Press, 2007.

Films

The Disenchanted Forest, Bullfrog Films, 2002. An award-winning film about returning rehabilitated orangutans to the wild.

Life of Mammals. BBC TV series hosted by David Attenborough. DVD.

Be the Creature. National Geographic Channel, 2004. The Kratt brothers take you to animal habitats around the world. DVD.

Web Sites

www.savegporangutans.org. Cheryl Knott's Gunung Palung Orangutan Conservation Program.

www.orangutan.net; www.sumatranorangutan.org; www.aim.uzh.ch/orangutannetwork; www.nationalgeographic.com/field/ explorers/cheryl-knott.html; www.nationalgeographic.com/ research/grantee/96/kntlmn.html; www.greatapetrust.org; www.fas.harvard.edu/~gporang/knott

INDEX

Boldface *indicates illustrations.*

Apes, compared to monkeys 6
Arboreal, definition 30

Canopy, definition 30
Climbing skills 10–12
Communication 12

Diet 6, **7, 9, 11**, 12, 28, 29

Endangered, definition 30

Facts at a glance 28–29
Families 15–16, **17, 20, 24–25,**
    25, 29
Feet 11, **28**
Females 9, 15–16, 17, 28, 29
Fighting 19
Food 6, **7, 9, 11**, 12, 28, 29

Glossary 30

Habitat 21–22, 25, 29, 30
Hands 10–11, **26**
Hormone, definition 30
How you can help 26

Infants **14**, 15, 16, **17, 20**

Jari Manus (orangutan) **4**, 5–7, **7**

Learning 19, 23, 25
Lifespan 28
Logging **21**, 21–22, **22**, 25

Males 17, **18**, 19, 28, 29
Mammals, definition 30
Map 10
Monkeys, compared to apes 6
Mothers **14**, 15, 16, **17, 20**

Nests **8,** 19

Orangutan, meaning of word 6
Orphans **20, 23,** 25

Pets 20
Population 28
Pregnancy **9**, 15–16

Range map 10
Rehabilitation centers 22–23, **23,**
    25, 30
Reproduction **9**, 15–16, 29
Research 17

Size 28
Social behavior 16, 19, 29
Solitary, definition 30
Sounds 12
Species 10, 28, 30

Termites 6, 7
Threats 29
Tool use 4, 6, 19, 28

Umbrella made from leaves **4**, 6
Urine 12–13, **13**, 15

Zoos 26, 27

RESEARCH & PHOTOGRAPHIC NOTES

Photographing and researching wild orangutans in the rain forest is a challenge, but we like it. We get to spend long days outdoors and to see not only orangutans, but also other amazing wildlife. Some things are hard, like waking up before daylight to hike in the dark to where the orangutan is sleeping so you can be there before they get up. Also, working in the rain forest means putting up with leeches, mosquitoes, and a lot of rain and wet boots. But it's worth it.

To get pictures of wild orangutans acting in a natural way, you first have to get them comfortable with you. Even if they are already used to a researcher, a big camera lens might make them nervous. If you take pictures from the ground looking up at orangutans in the trees, the photos often don't turn out well because of the bright sky background. So I tend to follow orangutans when they are in steep, hilly areas. I scramble up hills so that I can look across at their level, carrying a big, bright, 300 mm f2.8 lens and my camera. Because there isn't much light in the rain forest, I use a tripod to keep the camera steady.

It's hard to find a gap in the leaves and set up a shot while the orangutan is doing something interesting. Some days I follow one for 12 hours and don't get a single picture. That's frustrating. But other times I am rewarded by a great image of their behavior. I also rig up ropes and climb trees to get to their level. This works best at the big fruit trees where I know they'll visit often.

Cheryl became interested in studying great apes because she was curious about human evolution. Great apes are our closest relatives, so learning more about how the environment shaped their evolution can help us understand our own past as well. But orangutans are hard to find and follow, so Cheryl always works with a big team of Indonesian scientists, students, and field assistants. Her research also inspired her to help protect the orangutan's rain forest home. Her organization, the Gunung Palung Orangutan Conservation Program, works with people and institutions in Indonesia to accomplish this. As a Professor of Anthropology at Boston University she also teaches people about orangutans, apes, and human evolution.

We still have a lot to learn about orangutans and how to protect their remaining habitat. We hope that one day you will join us in the effort!

—TL

WE DEDICATE THIS BOOK TO OUR CHILDREN, RUSSELL AND JESSICA, WHO HAVE ENTHUSIASTICALLY ACCOMPANIED US TO BORNEO TO SEE WILD ORANGUTANS. ALSO, WE WOULD LIKE TO MAKE A SPECIAL DEDICATION TO THE CHILDREN OF INDONESIA AND MALAYSIA, WHO ARE THE KEY TO THE ORANGUTAN'S FUTURE. —TL & CK

Acknowledgments
We are grateful to the many institutions in Indonesia that have sponsored our research and fieldwork: The Indonesian Institute of Sciences, State Ministry of Research and Technology, Center for Research and Development in Biology, Indonesian Nature Conservation Service, Gunung Palung National Park Office, and Universitas Tanjungpura. Thank you to the field assistants, research assistants, and other collaborators who assisted us in our work at Gunung Palung. Tim thanks the National Geographic Society for supporting his research and photographic work in Indonesia over many years. Cheryl also thanks the many organizations that have supported her research and conservation work—including, among others, National Geographic Society; National Science Foundation; Leakey Foundation; Conservation, Food, and Health Foundation; U.S. Fish and Wildlife Service; and Orangutan Conservancy.

Finally, we thank our parents for their encouragement and support of our travels to Indonesia over the years, for instilling in us a belief that we could accomplish whatever we wanted to, and for inspiring a life-long interest in learning.
                    —Tim Laman and Cheryl Knott

Book design by David M. Seager. The body text of the book is set in ITC Century. The display text is set in Knockout and Party Noid.

Published by the
National Geographic Society

John M. Fahey, Jr., *President and Chief Executive Officer*

Gilbert M. Grosvenor, *Chairman of the Board*

Tim T. Kelly, *President, Global Media Group*

John Q. Griffin, *President, Publishing*

Nina D. Hoffman, *Executive Vice President; President, Book Publishing Group*

Staff for This Book

Nancy Laties Feresten, *Vice President, Editor-in-Chief of Children's Books*

Bea Jackson, *Design and Illustrations Director, Children's Books*

Amy Shields, *Executive Editor*

Jennifer Emmett, Mary Beth Oelkers-Keegan, *Project Editors*

David M. Seager, *Art Director*

Lori Epstein, *Illustrations Editor*

Jocelyn G. Lindsay, *Researcher*

Connie Binder, *Indexer*

Carl Mehler, *Director of Maps*

Rebecca Baines, *Assistant Editor*

Jennifer Thornton, *Managing Editor*

Grace Hill, *Associate Managing Editor*

R. Gary Colbert, *Production Director*

Lewis R. Bassford, *Production Manager*

Nicole Elliott, *Manufacturing Manager*

Susan Borke, *Legal and Business Affairs*

The publisher gratefully acknowledges the assistance of Christine Kiel, K-3 curriculum and reading consultant; and for his assistance with the map, Erik Meijaard, PhD, Senior Scientist and OCSP Conservation Strategy Specialist.

Library of Congress Cataloging-in-Publication Data

Laman, Tim. Face to face with orangutans / by Tim Laman & Cheryl Knott.
   p. cm.
Includes bibliographical references and index.
ISBN 978-1-4263-0464-4 (hardcover: alk. paper)—ISBN 978-1-4263-0465-1 (library binding: alk. paper)
1. Orangutan—Juvenile literature. I. Knott, Cheryl Denise. II. Title.   QL737.P96L344 2009 599.88'3—dc22

                              2009000170

Founded in 1888, the National Geographic Society is one of the largest nonprofit scientific and educational organizations in the world. It reaches more than 285 million people worldwide each month through its official journal, NATIONAL GEOGRAPHIC, and its four other magazines; the National Geographic Channel; television documentaries; radio programs; films; books; videos and DVDs; maps; and interactive media. National Geographic has funded more than 8,000 scientific research projects and supports an education program combating geographic illiteracy.

For more information, please call 1-800-NGS LINE (647-5463) or write to the following address:

National Geographic Society
1145 17th Street N.W.
Washington, D.C. 20036-4688 U.S.A.

Visit us online at www.nationalgeographic.com/books. Librarians and teachers, visit us at www.ngchildrensbooks.org. Kids and parents, visit us at kids.nationalgeographic.com.

For information about special discounts for bulk purchases, please contact National Geographic Books Special Sales: ngspecsales@ngs.org. For rights or permissions inquiries, please contact National Geographic Books Subsidiary Rights: ngbookrights@ngs.org.

Printed in USA

Front cover & pages 2–3: Face to face with an orangutan in Borneo. *Front flap:* A juvenile orangutan. *Back cover:* A long-armed orangutan drops in for a visit and nabs some fruit. *Page 1:* An orangutan uses his long arms and feet, pulling himself from branch to branch.